entre ríos books

www.entreriosbooks.com
Seattle, Washington

ORANGE
Copyright ©2020 E. Briskin

ISBN: 978-0-9600457-1-6

First Edition. ERB 011.
Printed in the United States.

Our books are proudly distributed by:

Small Press Distribution
www.spdbooks.org
800.869.7553.

COVER ILLUSTRATION
Briton Riviere, wood engraving in Charles Darwin's
The Expression of the Emotions in Man and Animals, 1872.

Go on

495
over. Back

496
up back up.

494

It's not —

497

Dogs don't like to back up, unless they're tugging

493

You died, and it has altered my stance, your stance.

498

a sleeve, a rope.

1

My dog died today.
It was unexpected.
One hour it was barking
then it stopped.

I am used to having something
this size
in my house
making noises
disturbing my sleep.
I have books and a speaker
blankets
bones on the floor.
Why can't things keep going
as they were?

492

You died. It was an imposition.

499

It's part play bow:

2

My dog died today.
Definitely not
yesterday.

The driver was a kid and his text said "hamburgers!"

White bumper.
Red splatter.
Tufts of fur.

491

Something large seized the withers of my soul.

500

forepaws bent, haunches up.

3

My dog died today
mostly metaphorically.
Not that she didn't
but that he hadn't
been alive.
I don't want to talk about

results of electrocardiogram
Let's play
twenty questions. Is it mineral?
Is it mammal? No, don't answer. Is it
a dog?

490

You died. No, you didn't. You departed.

501

The way dogs stalk up slowly, stealthily.

4

My dog died today
allegorically.
Not that it didn't
but that it left
the world to live.

489

You died. All my conscience won't return you.

502

It's not stealthy, not at all.

5

My dog died today.
My friends have tired
of it. That
fuzz-wiry rat thing?
Gozzled shine beast?
Mud-tailed drooler?
Was that even a dog?

488

I don't know.

503

Like Orson Welles in *Touch of Evil*, hiding plainly behind a slender pole.

6

My dog died today, and tomorrow and Wednesday.
Twenty years ago you
are still dead.

487

A dog, in this construction, is *sort of* conscious.[1] Does this
construct change the nature of my loss?

504

Last night, I was reading more about you. How Linnaeus clas-
sified species by teeth.[2]

---

1   Joshua Rothman, "Daniel Dennett's Science of the Soul," *New Yorker,* March 27, 2017. Rothman conveying Dennett: "The obvious answer to the question of whether animals have selves is that they sort of have them." https://www.newyorker.com/magazine/2017/03/27/daniel-dennetts-science-of-the-soul.

2   "Linnaeus counted teeth, which is one reason why he put dogs, wolves, coyotes, jackals, and dingoes in the same genus, *Canis.*" Raymond Coppinger and Lorna Coppinger, *What Is a Dog?* (Chicago: The University of Chicago Press, 2016), 6.

7
My dog died today.
I don't miss it.
There's the cleanup to do.

Then I'll go out.

486
Dennett believes — if I'm understanding — that consciousness
is materialist — made of functions. Like if you turn on enough
functions, selfhood happens.[3]

505
If I added a few teeth — would it change me? I have 31. You: 42.
Eleven more.

---

3 Rothman on Dennett in the *New Yorker*: "It was possible, [Dennett]
said, to be 'neutral about the metaphysical status of the data.' From the
outside, it looks like neurons; from the inside, it feels like consciousness.
Problem solved[?]"

8

My dog died today
which is a thing that isn't
true.
It was more of an insect
than a dog
which is a thing that isn't
true. A thought is
more an insect than
a dog.

485

But dogs have part of the awareness of a creature that knows
itself. Daniel Dennett is a philosopher that I know of from —[4]

506

If I, born a woman (except I wasn't? why think I was?). If I, from
utero with utero, can become something else, is a dog such

---

4   *Aeon*? Nope. Ibid. I checked.

9

My dog, who was a spider,
died yesterday.
I was restless at night.
Its legs were hairy. I
crushed it. I got up to get
myself a little drink.

484

When we talk of a dog nearby dogs' ears prick up. They don't
worry, though, what we're saying about them. Whether we
think they are fetching or nice.

507

a faraway possibility? Why can't I add teeth to meet Linnaeus?
I could add a whatchamacallit organ[5] to my nose.

---

5 "There is some evidence that humans unconsciously perceive phero-
mones, perhaps even through a nasal vomeronasal organ.*" [The * is to a
footnote about Martha McClintock.] "Dogs definitely have a vomeronasal
organ: it sits above the roof (hard palate) of the mouth, along the floor of
the nose (nasal septum)." Alexandra Horowitz, *Inside of a Dog: What Dogs
See, Smell, and Know* (New York: Scribner, 2010), 73–74.

10

My dog, had it existed, would
die today. I can tell because the sky
looks like grey gum.

483

Because wolves have to pull apart bodies. They drag them over
snow or into forests, away from wolves.

508

I would need to add olfactory receptors. (Could a cell be
implanted?) 215 million?[6]

---

6 "The average person has around 5 million scent receptors in his
or her nose ... The average dog has around 220 million receptors in its
nose ..." Stanley Coren, *How to Speak Dog: Mastering the Art of Dog–Human
Communication* (New York: Atria Paperback, 2014), 183.

11

My dog.

482

One experiment was vaguely: Pull this rope, pull that rope, pull this other one. The wolves all learned faster than the dogs.[7]

509

If only I had dogged ears.

---

7   "Hand-raised wolves tested on their ability to learn a task — to pull three ropes from an array of ropes in a particular order — well outperformed the dogs tested." Horowitz, *Inside of a Dog*, 44.

12

My dog died today. This isn't a borscht belt routine.

It didn't dye its ears or its tuchus or a hind claw. It didn't four-foot over some Rubicon. It wasn't reborn as the mother of the father of all of Rome.

481

I read those books a little. I mean: I read them. One of the advantages of wolves over dogs: A wolf can learn to pull ropes in a particular pattern.

510

I want the kind you had — determined.

13

My dog died today and before my dog died it had a few things to say.

I don't know.

480

If a dog read, what would it enjoy reading? Strategies for food procurement. Signs that person's almost home. Ways to lower a car's windows until they disappear.

511

Which way did they go: Down or up?

14

My dog died today and not yesterday.
Not the day before.
Today: Dead dog.

479

I haven't read them I haven't read them today I read them.

512

15

My dog died today
out of boredom.
It was tired of hearing
which day it died.

478

Unless I stop now — stop writing — I'll finish writing
before I finish reading. You finished. Here are books — not
esoteric — about your life.

— *The Other End of the Leash*
— *Inside of a Dog*
— *How to Speak Dog*
— *What Is a Dog?*
— *The Dog: A Natural History*
— *I Am Not a Brain*
— *The Future of the Mind*
— *Intuition Pumps*

513

About time. Does a year feel the same to us?

16

My dog died today. What does that mean
even? "My" dog.

477

To my left, two women are talking. They are friends with a
person who has my name. Now I listen to them the way you
would. I hear sound mumbles, and then, "Puppy!" and then
sound mumbles and then, "Puppy!" Each puppy turns my head.
Every. Time.

514

Out the window of the coffee shop a woman is walking her
husky.

17

My dog, which is to say a dog that lived on my couch, died today, which is to say a sofa dog stopped living. This happened today, which Samuel Johnson defines as the time of light that is happening in the present.[8]

476

Although a dog playing with a toy will still be focused on its owner. A hand holds the future. Jacket? Treat.

515

His hair and her cockles stand straight up.

---

8   He doesn't. The entries in the edition of his dictionary I consulted skip from "TOD" (second definition: "A certain weight of wool, twenty-eight pounds.") to "TOE" ("The divided extremities of the feet; the fingers of the feet.").

Samuel Johnson, *A Dictionary of the English Language: In Which the Words Are Deduced from Their Originals, and Illustrated in Their Different Significations by Examples from the Best Writers*, 6th ed., vol. 2 (London, 1785). Accessed at: https://archive.org/details/dictionaryofengl02johnuoft.

18

My dog died today, and all night I keep walking the curbs, grabbing dog shit, dangling collars from my hand.

475

A dog is the opposite of a child, I am thinking. A dog playing with a toy is a dog playing with a toy. Total focus without bids for attention.

516

You died.

19

My dog died today, and it turns out that no dog is not the same thing as one dog no longer.

A study suggests we become accustomed, very quickly, to the good in our lives.[9] We feel bereft when that good passes on.

This fur tuft — remove it! It fetches memories.

Or will I miss it after I ~~delete~~ lint-roll it away?

474

Now he's leaving, and says, "Bye-bye." He holds a muffin in his hands. When his dad stuffs the bear into the toy crate, he pays no mind.

517

Today was so long ago.

---

9   Philip Brickman, Dan Coates, and Ronnie Janoff-Bulman, "Lottery Winners and Accident Victims: Is Happiness Relative?," *Journal of Personality and Social Psychology* 36, no. 8 (1978): 917–27. https://doi.org/10.1037/0022-3514.36.8.917.

20

When your dog dies
the world decides
to divide itself into two:
the world of people
who understand grief
and those who don't.[10]

473

He tells me the bear's a baby that he saved from the toy crate.
I look over. The crate holds two alligators. Brave guy.

518

All those thoughts twisted in grief.

---

10 I thought this was a reference to a Dorothy Parker quote, but it was Robert Benchley who wrote: "There may be said to be two classes of people in the world; those who constantly divide the people of the world into two classes, and those who do not."

Vanity Fair's Book Reviewer [Benchley], "The Most Popular Book of the Month: An Extremely Literary Review of the Latest Edition of the New York City Telephone Directory," *Vanity Fair*, February 1920, 69. https://babel.hathitrust.org/cgi/pt?id=mdp.39015032024203;seq=203.

Source for reference: Quote Investigator — https://quoteinvestigator.com/2014/02/07/two-classes.

21

Where's your come-back-soon-now heartbreak whine?

472

He keeps putting it on his head and then yelling: "He climbed on my head. He climbed on my head AGAIN!"

519

Was there a minute in the last eight hours when I didn't think dog, dog? When I didn't brush my hand out for your chest?

22

Where's your ear pricked
for the click of claws?

471

Next table over at the shop where I'm writing: a little boy hold-
ing a small-eared, enormous-footed, brown-eyed bear.

520

If I became one of your species, there's the matter of fur.

23

Some of my friends have the mistaken impression that my dog
must have been very large.

470

First this snippet from my memory. Is it memory that makes
pain?

521

Surely there's a dog version of Rogaine® out there somewhere.

24

Once, due to complicated circumstances, a dog I loved didn't
see me for two years

469

This is long and I'm thinking of how my fingers will respond.
Repetition. Fetch the ball. Fetch. Drop.

522

Surely somewhere is a full-body wig of fur.

25

and still when I entered his new
apartment building, he heard/smelled me
through a door from the end of a long hall
and he howled his me howl and he danced
his me dance.[11] I'm not saying that's
what happened, but that's
how it went.[12]

468

To miss play is to miss joy. I miss [keepworking] my [keep-
working] dog.

523

If I were you, my day would not change much. The same walk-
ing. Some more napping. Constant snacks.

---

11   Sendak, RIP.

12   This did happen, more or less. It also happened, after a much
longer absence (~seven years), to a hound named Flannel and a WWII
vet named Stephen Birch: "'He did his little dance and sounded off with
that "Woo-woo" song of his.'" Stanley Coren, *How Dogs Think: What the
World Looks Like to Them and Why They Act the Way They Do* (New York:
Free Press, 2005), 275–76.

26

It's not that I don't believe in coincidence. It's that I believe in my dog.

467

Last night Lassie and I played her favorite game together.[13]

524

I might have more success finding catch partners. Is it easy to catch with a mouth?

---

13   Patricia B. McConnell, *For the Love of a Dog: Understanding Emotion in You and Your Best Friend* (New York: Ballantine Books Trade Paperback Edition, 2007), 287.

This reminds me of an earlier quote: "I am not afraid to admit that my nature is so tender, so childish, that I cannot well refuse my dog the play he offers me or asks of me outside the proper time."

Michel de Montaigne, *Michel de Montaigne: The Complete Works* [late 16th century], trans. Donald M. Frame (New York: Everyman's Library, 2003), 385.

27

You really think your dog is the "warmest fuzziest"?

Your dog's half a dew-
claw to my dog.

466

A human craves immortality,[14] a dog just wants to play. To hurtle itself against your person. To mock-sink its teeth into a friend's fur. To catch the ball more times than you can throw.

525

I saw a video once of a chihuahua that peed during paw-stands.

---

14   Source: Everything ever written.

28

My dog died and the grey squirrel sleeps unnoticed.

465

And now I'm thinking about how much of socialization is an enthusiasm sink. I've forgotten what I was saying here. What day is this?

526

The message it left on the lamppost: I'm tall.

29

O thin dogs of Haddam,[15] watch and bay for my dog.

464

My friend died of embarrassment.

527

Alexandra Horowitz compares hydrants to bulletin boards.[16]
Tattered posters, ripping time, decaying scent. Deterioration is

---

15 This line, except for the part where I've swapped "men" for "dogs," is
from Wallace Stevens's "Thirteen Ways of Looking at a Blackbird," stanza 7.

16 "...with old, deteriorating announcements and requests peeking out
from underneath more recent posts of activities and successes." Horowitz,
Inside of a Dog, 84.

30

Once, late at night, the toilet seat lid flipped down, crashing.
Who went apeshit-kill-the-burglar?
My dog.

463

to be delighted by a rude dog?

528

wisdom. Information, I guess. Even before you sniff the subject
you smell how faint it is.[17]

---

17   I have John Berger in mind here. See footnote 70.

31

Those red rocks in your yard look so pretty. Who would eat
them like roses?
Guess.

462

One guy yanked his beard and made pebble eyes at us, accept-
ing my friend's apology through sucked lips. Is it wrong

529

I think about it sometimes like gossip. "Zoe's pregnant!" says
the spaniel, her nose at the fence. "She smells wonderful! I didn't
know."

32

If I had had a cat then this wouldn't be happening. A cat lives forever. Not my dog.

461

A few of the fathers stormed and stomped.

530

The problem is, how does he say it? How does a dog mention what they know?

33

My friends have suggested I get over my dog. "Have this puppy," they say. That's not a dog.

460

The dog would look one way furtively, or perhaps as if recalling something, then turn back, and, like lightning, like upside-down lightning, starting at a flea-sized chin dimple, lickitsface. Most of the mothers found this funny.

531

Have I ever — I wonder — met a dog I didn't like? There was Artie's dog: brutal, unfriendly.[18] Always longing to lunge through window glass.

---

18   "Art is the setting-into-work of truth." Martin Heidegger, *Poetry, Language, Thought*, trans. Albert Hofstadter (New York: Harper Perennial Modern Thought, 2013), 74.

34

And now there's a puppy on my sofa. It can't get down on its
own off the furniture. It isn't made up of thick wool. It's a silk
thread at best, and the wrong tone — the wrong smell. It might
be a mammal. Not a dog.

459

Whenever it saw a baby it would try to lick its cheeks.

532

Thinking back, Artie's boyfriend was similar. Brooding.
Thudding forward through the force of complaints.

35

I can't give a name to the puppy. Names are things that belong to my dog.

458

It had spent its puppyhood in a home day care.

533

Art's next love was work-minded and forgetful.

36

A nightmare tonight. My dog glared, ripped my throat. Growled whale-eyed on top of my chest.

457

She had a dog once — a golden retriever.

534

Would you choose to be subjected to a sulky, cold neglect?

37

This puppy can't even hold its own bladder. Who pees on some-one's sweater? Not my dog.

456

She doesn't know it, but I send half-formed thoughts.

535

Or would you rather be absent-professored from existence?

38

Patricia McConnell suggests that animus between dogs can arise from the inadvertent behaviors of their owners.[19] Is that why this puppy nipped that beagle? How dare it eyeball me. It's not my dog.

455

A friend of mine from long, long ago is still my friend although we never meet or talk.

536

Dogs aren't like that, or when they are it looks different.

---

19   Please read Patricia B. McConnell's *The Other End of the Leash: Why We Do What We Do Around Dogs* (New York: Ballantine Books, 2003).

Also, see this small study about emotions:

Natalia Albuquerque, Kun Guo, Anna Wilkinson, Carine Savalli, Emma Otta, and Daniel Mills, "Dogs Recognize Dog and Human Emotions," *Biology Letters* 12 (2016). https://doi.org/10.1098/rsbl.2015.0883.

39

I think I will give the little puppy to a friend.

454

Even for a dog, your smile is succinctly blinding. So many teeth, so much said around the eyes.

537

(I'm contradicting a similarity I just discussed.)

40

If my dog lived in '40s France would it be fascist? Do we begrudge Gertrude and Basket II their gentle war?

A dog is like a physicist who cannot live without doing physics and doesn't ask itself what that physics will bring about.

To run — it is good.
To growl at strangers — also good.[20]
To bite into intruders — good, good.

453

When I want to forget, I can't stop[21] this. Every thought is your forehead. Every leash is your leash. Each bark sails from the cove of your chest.

538

Outside the shop: strange men staring in at me. It's creepy, and I glare, then ignore them, but I'd go out to pet them, if they were dogs.

---

20   Also, not good. See, for example:

Tyler Parry, "Police Dogs and Anti-Black Violence," *African American Intellectual History Society*, July 31, 2017. https://www.aaihs.org/police-dogs-and-anti-black-violence.

21   "...Toby, —— stop! — go not one foot further..." Laurence Sterne, *The Life and Opinions of Tristram Shandy, Gentleman* [1759 to 1767] (New York: Penguin Classics, 1985), 110.

41

Last night I was dreaming and then woke up to soft fur — rough and yellow at the top of my foot fingers. I reached out my hand and ruffled empty gold. Good dog, my sleep voice chortled. Oh, good dog.

452

And me with my scent-blunted nose. I can't smell you. To remember, I wear wool in rain.

539

Last night I read something amazing about your breed. But what was it?

Will I forget the way your head wags?

(&&&)

42

Why have I
been abandoned
by my dog?

451

Like a scent-map of my previous week or weeks.[22]

540

---

22   Horowitz cites a study in which dogs accurately recognized the scent of a fingerprint on a slide that had been on a rooftop for several days. Horowitz, *Inside of a Dog*, 78.

I think the study she refers to is this one:

J. Edward King, R. Frederick Becker, and J. E. Markee, "Studies on Olfactory Discrimination in Dogs: (3) Ability to Detect Human Odour Trace," *Animal Behaviour* 12, no. 2–3 (April–July 1964): 311–15. https://doi.org/10.1016/0003-3472(64)90017-X.

(These sources describe scent, not maps.)

43

Newish science news, if that's what you call this type of thing:
Dogs are relaxed by music — different kinds, different dogs.[23]

Did you know that dogs feel splinters and the sun?

450

So much information is the decision of the wind. But I thought,
if you were here, you'd know everywhere I'd been.

541

The puppy at the coffee shop plays with a squeaky bird until
the bird tumbles outside the half-circle of the pup's leash. The
pup whines and cries while its people (business talking) ignore
it. I shift my weight, point my toe, and kick the bird gently. It
tumbles squeaking into the puppy's toothy reach.

---

23   A. Bowman, Scottish SPCA, F. J. Dowell, and N. P. Evans, "The Effect
of Different Genres of Music on the Stress Levels of Kennelled Dogs,"
Physiology & Behavior 171 (March 15, 2017): 207–15. https://doi.org/
10.1016/j.physbeh.2017.01.024.

44

My dog died today, and a man in a black Utilikilt hovers nearby. He's here with his husband, who wears a Utilikilt of many colors and is salvaging a coffee-sodden board game.

449

Scent can be blocked by a tree trunk.

542

I expect this to become a drop-whine-return game, but it doesn't.

45

My dog died today but the news I read was about humans.
My dog. My poor still dead dog.

448

Of the gas or the diesel. Of bay rum.

543

It's the ball returned to play at the tennis court, not the cup
dropped from a high chair 200 times.

46

One afternoon I got home early and my dog was on the sofa and my dog is not allowed there so it squiggled itself forward until its front paws were on the carpet and looked up like, "WhatI'mNotOnYourSofaWhat?"

447

I thought of me driving it and you beside me. The smell of each leaf, and of the wind.

544

The pup is restless. Every time I look up, it's in a different posture, different place. Now sitting on the toy. Now wriggling beneath it. Now hugging the toy in its paws.

47

Sometimes my dog just didn't like someone. That someone might be saintlike or a mensch. I didn't let that prospect matter. Do not take it into account. If you don't trust your dog, there's no dog.

446

I thought of you driving the pickup, somehow, nosing over from your customary seat.

545

I had a friend once who had the focus of a puppy.

48

My dog died today, and so has robbed me of my dog, which is fitting, as my dog was an inveterate thief: a robber baron if not the Red Baron like that Snoopy fellow. Belongings were in peril when her mouth was empty. Then the stuffed bear, the worn bone, the electrical cord became not tempting so much as quickly hers.

445

The leaves rustled and turned like a storm was coming. Which, I guess in some senses, it was.

546

Each blink opened the curtains to a new act.

49

On a website I fall into, a commenter hypothesizes that an average-sized dog sheds thirty pounds of fur over a fourteen-year lifetime. My dog was slightly smaller than average, and he died before she lived fourteen years. Let's say they shed roughly seven pounds of fur, two pounds of it in parks and on walks. Let's assume my vacuum isn't fantastic: There must be a half pound of fur in my house. Half of it in this room. There is still more of her.

444

from the top.

547

It didn't last.

50

There's a border collie named Chaser who knows the words for 1,022 things.[24] Her owner, Dr. Pilley,[25] says that training Chaser healed his heart.[26] He also says dogs are distressed by arguments. Did my dog know the word for sofa?

Sorry?

443

I was looking at the canopy —

548

A dog can be so good at noticing things — what you're holding, how you're moving, when you stop. When you've slept with one person, then another, then the first, or when your friend left the park before you showed up.[27]

---

24   John W. Pilley and Alliston K. Reid, "Border Collie Comprehends Object Names as Verbal Referents," *Behavioural Processes* 86, no. 2 (February 2011): 184–95. https://doi.org/10.1016/j.beproc.2010.11.007.

25   July 1, 1928–June 17, 2018. RIP.

26   "...mending Dr Pilley's heart, which had shattered after the death of his dog Yasha in the 1990s."

Lydia Warren, "Want Your Dog to Be as Clever as Chaser [...]?," *Daily Mail*, December 4, 2013. Accessed at: http://www.dailymail.co.uk/news/article-2514700/Owner-taught-dog-A-THOUSAND-words-shares-secrets-success.html.

27   See Horowitz, *Inside of a Dog*, 79, for the spirit of this section.

51

My dog was kind, but he wasn't unbiased.

She liked people who were poorly or immaculately dressed.

Ah, cologne.

442

Yesterday I drove behind a white pickup truck with a tree in the back, horizontal with its top hanging over the gate.

549

A dog's tail, when its dog sees a loved one, tends to wag harder and more often to the right.[28] Did yours tend the way I think?

---

28   Horowitz, *Inside of a Dog*, 113.

A. Quaranta, M. Siniscalchi, and G. Vallortigara, "Asymmetric Tail-Wagging Responses by Dogs to Different Emotive Stimuli," *Current Biology* 17, no. 6 (March 20, 2007): 199–201. http://doi.org/10.1016/j.cub.2007.02.008.

"When faced with their owner...dogs exhibited a striking right-sided bias in the amplitudes of tail wagging..."

52

Domain:	Eukarya	Class:	Mammalia
Kingdom:	Animalia	Order:	Carnivora
Phylum:	Chordata	Family:	Canidae
Subphylum:	Vertebrata	Genus:	*Canis*

Species:	*Canis lupus*
Subspecies:	*Canis lupus familiaris*[29]

Breed:	Withholding
Name:	Withheld

From Old English *docga*. Closest living relative: gray wolf. I am also the closest relation to my dog.

441

Grief isn't a fucking corporate meeting, I wish she'd said. You mean, what did we learn at the despair retreat.

550

I can't picture it now. I am sluggish. So tired. Dog. Dog. Dog.

---

29   This is not without controversy. Scientists using an ecological definition rather than a biological one stick with Linnaeus's name: *Canis familiaris*. Ádám Miklósi, Tamás Faragó, Claudia Fugazza, Márta Gácsi, Enikö [*sic*] Kubinyi, Péter Pongrácz, and József Topál, *The Dog: A Natural History* (Princeton, NJ: Princeton University Press, 2018), 30.

53

The Highland wild dog isn't extinct, after all.[30]

440

She was just two days into a breakup and someone had already asked her what she'd learned.

551

Is this day still carrying on with its day stuff?

30   New Guinea Highland Wild Dog Foundation Den Site (blog), "New Guinea Highland Wild Dog Discovery Press Release: The NGHWDF is pleased to announce the re-discovery of the New Guinea Highland Wild Dog," March 2, 2017. http://www.nghwdf.org/the-den-site/welcome-to-our-blog-but-what-is-it.

54

Let time be

439

After, on the bus home, my friend said to me —

552

I could swear the sun set so many times.

55

a navigable distance.

438

He had lost her. And these songs — they refused to make meaning from loss.

553

After Raymond Queneau:[31]

Outside the café a man stood at the window making his arms into a hoop. His dog leapt up through the hoop, and then waited. In a second, he was eating a treat. Then the man put his hoop into separate pockets. He walked into the café. I'd like two Americanos, he said.

---

31   The part after this is in the style of *Exercises in Style*. Raymond Queneau, *Exercises in Style*, trans. Barbara Wright (New York: New Directions, 2012).

56

On the ferry to Bainbridge Island the machine's out of coffee.
Just as well. I don't want to wake up.

437

One song for each year he had spent with his wife.

554

Outside the café was a man with arms making a hoop. He gave
a treat to a dog that jumped through after leaping up. Then he
walked into the shop with his hands in his pockets. He said,
"I'd like an Americano. I'd like two."

57

The ferry doors open and the wind makes a whistle. I have watched how your tail moves when sound stops.

436

Last night I heard a man spend an hour on grief. I paid $16.50 to hear thirteen songs.

555

It was about ten in the morning somewhere in the Pacific Northwest. A few paces from the door a man of middle to old age stood with his extremities spread moderately widely apart. He had a youngish, medium-sized dog with him. He formed his arms into a shape like a hoop or a ring. His dog, or some-body's, jumped up — or sort of bounced — through the more or less middle of the hoopish shape. One of the dog's back legs may have brushed or kicked the man's forearm or maybe struck against his shoulder or an elbow-pit — Go on.

58

The fact of a vacancy is a sort of nonfact. The sofa has a mild indentation. The water is low and stale in the bowl. I'll replace it — I replace it. I will fluff it. It's so plump. It is fresh now. It's so fresh. Come here. Come.

435

You stopped.

556

When we went out, how many people you knew whom I didn't. When did you all meet? You knew someone on every walk. Hi, _____, they'd smile, their voice chiming with your name. I'd look up for a tight little nod.

59

I had a friend once, I mean someone I worked with, who'd ask me sometimes, "Will you be my dog?" He wanted to sound out an idea while I listened; no response.

434

Am I stopping? For the moment? No.

557

No one mentions how grief feels from the inside. Or I haven't listened and everyone does.

60

The first day I met him was his first day on the job. He almost quit during a meeting on transition plans: It was packed full of "hit by a bus" jokes. His mother was hit by a bus. No.

433

Dropped umbrella, dragging coat-belt, coffee splash:

> my boss.

I had tensed to the tumble of her.

558

So, what does it feel like? A convulsion. Collapsed trench.

61

No. No joke. Now I think of those things — listening and mothers — together. A mother reflects back the ways you exist. Careful attention, without judgment, accepting everything.

432

I was at a film festival that lasted several weeks. As I leaned over the balcony my mind sensed a disturbance. I still remember how it registered — as chaos erupting. I looked down.

559

If a blanket could drape like a punch.

62

All of us need someone to be our dog.

431

If the devil's in the details, she had no devil, not at all. Once I was at the balcony of a movie theatre, in a mall —

560

The punch blanket spreads unexpectedly. There's what I was doing — look, *I'm doing so well!* Look at me walking by the dog park without (ANGUISH) never mind.

63

I seek cartoons for comfort — but not Disney: those iconic dogs of slobber and shallow mind.

430

But looking at it all now, through this mystery, I feel tender towards her valiant attempts at organization, and her capitalization of the words Right Good Truth.

561

And now all the people who ask about you. Where's Dog today? Dog not feeling it? Hey, loser! You forgot to bring Dog!

64

Was it Warner Brothers who had the Road Runner? That foiled coyote. In life, a coyote can run more than 42 miles per hour. A roadrunner tops out shy of 20 mph.[32]

429

I once knew a woman who dropped things. My boss. She played her position like a butterfingered shortstop. She'd ignore emails for years and then answer them chronologically. We'd get answers to questions from the twentieth century. I remember being sucked thin with contempt for her.

562

The dog asked, too, at first, if you were absent. It doesn't need to ask now. Your fainted smell.

---

32 http://speedofanimals.com.

65

My dog — oh, forget it — I don't have a dog. No leash has ever hung on this brass hook. That low bed, so cozy — what's it doing here? And this clutch of fur, too coarse to be mine.

428

There's a woman called "the woman who dropped things." Such a woman, I imagine, you would like.

563

I almost don't want to tell you, as I've told you already, but there's this guy with a dog and the dog can do tricks and every morning the dog does them in front of a café.

66

I hear, fairly often, about dogs that take baths. They sound nice, but do they smell doggy? Here, dog.

427

Everything about it — if this type of escape suits you — is perfect. Witty dialogue, gender confusions, open fun. Ridiculous insults lobbed at a Cantabrigian[33] by an Oxonian.[34] The word "Strewth!"[35] is — at least once — deployed.

564

The day was blue white, and a man who was white pink stood in front of a streaked window with a white dog that was black in brown shadows. The man wore a green grey shirt and a pair of red musk pants. The dog's mouth, when it opened, was pink black with clear spittle. The dog jumped, and its shadow cast the sidewalk from taupe to tan.

---

33   Cambridge student or grad.

34   Student or graduate of the University of Oxford.

35   "alteration of *God's truth*" — *Collins English Dictionary*, online.

67

Today, outside the bakery: a little grey dog, tiny Lab pup. I bend to pat it. It leaps inside my arms.

426

Not even the family of tennis players has a dog.

565

So there's this guy, right? Made of carbon, made of water, wearing fabric made of cotton, also plastic made of something else, and wool. And there's this dog, right? Made of carbon, made of water, wearing fur made out of something, maybe made out of the same thing — like itself? So this guy stands in front of a café made out of metal, also plastic, plaster, wood, and sheets of glass. He stands there on a sidewalk, and it's made of concrete, right? Made of aggregate and cement, plus made of time. And this guy shows his dog into a hole made out of nothing, with a show made out of food made out of sheep — of sheep and scraps.

68

Outside the café every weekday (how did the café get up here?), a man does tricks with his medium-sized dog. His arms form a distorted loop, and the dog leaps through it. I used to watch and think: What is performance? What's the line between an act and showing off?

425

There's a mystery I read every six years or so. It's good, I think, but there aren't any dogs in it.

566

Every day the same guy stood in front of a shop and did dog tricks for everyone's benefit. All that time all the customers were blocked from petting his soft friend.

He didn't really do dog tricks — he tricked his dog.

69

Today it's less performance than preening, I think. He has a dog who loves him. Yesterday, so did I.

424

Am I being unfair? You wouldn't ask yourself that. You'd snub treats from their hands, if they offered. I miss you. That's the point.[36]

567

Did I tell you about this? It was the coolest thing. This man, born in Tucson in 1956, every morning he takes his border collie to the café. He makes a hoop with his arms, about twenty-six inches wide, and then whistles once — A$^\sharp$ — and the dog jumps through. They complete twenty jumps in three and a half minutes. The dog is terrifically agile, and so is he. When you watch customers watching them you see people gasp with awe. He's a cool man with such a cool dog.

---

36 "'And why should not my cheeks be starved and my face drawn?'" In my copy of *The Epic of Gilgamesh*, Gilgamesh says this on page 101. Then he says it again (103, 105).

The Epic of Gilgamesh [~1700 BCE], trans. N. K. Sandars (Harmondsworth, Middlesex: Penguin Books, 1985), 101–5.

70

At the water in Canada, a dog dives after a stick. The dog's caught in a current, and its owner, a woman, sprints downstream. At a bend they draw close, and she lands the dog — reels her in. The dog is half dead, the owner beyond spent. They collapse on a path. A long panting pause, then the dog opens her mouth and the stick drops.

423

A church can be everything peaceful. But these two: I couldn't relax my thoughts with them around. The size of their vehicle was enormous. The pristine adventure fabric of their clothing set me on edge.

568

Jump
back.

71

I am no one without sticks for dogs.

422

If there is truth how would this guy know it? Next I heard them arguing about church finances.

569

(I am jealous here inside my own hoop.)

72

There's a green field nearby, an illicit dog park. There's this maple branch fat in my hand.

421

I mean really? Then her gentleman companion started talking in these phrases: "I could have told you that last year" and "that's the way it is" and "all I can tell you is the truth."

570

Outside a bench in front of a hedge and a hedge in front of a tree and in front of the bench a man with a dog in front of him and in front of the dog the man's rounded arms. The dog is between them. The arms and the man. The dog is performing in front of windows. The windows are in front of a café.

73

Have you heard that long story about dying? It always ends the same way. There's a woman, or maybe she's just a person. Her mom dies, then her brother or farther [*sic*] or someone, then her lover, and then her best friend. She holds up to these losses in a manner people "admire." [I want to channel Hollinghurst channeling Henry James here.[37] She implodes when she loses her dog.

420

I'm used to distraction, irritation. This was different. First the lady's just-made drink wasn't "nearly" hot enough. The barista made a new one. I thought, really?

571

This weekend, today, I went to a birthday party. Each balloon, every candle was a taunt.

---

37   But it's a quote I can't locate or recall.]

74

I know what you're thinking — that the dog held five griefs. But maybe grief for her dog was grief just for her dog. The grief she collapsed into was for her dog.

419

At the coffee shop I have the right pen again. The couple who just left have a bad vibe.

572

Three people told identical stories about their Labradoodles.

75

You think that's callow? I don't think so. Some of us have morning coffee as companions. Now try living a morning without coffee. Bereft. Now imagine your coffee was a dog.

418

Was it familiarity? Was it confidence? I won't explain.

573

Then a barista told me that she had a puppy, a Staffordshire. When she left it alone, it would chew things: shirt, shoe, laptop, doorjamb, fancy coats.

76

In 1940, a dog named Robot discovered the Lascaux paintings. Or teenagers did when they trailed their dog.[38] [39]

Did Amundsen reach the South Pole before his huskies did?[40]

417

"Thank you, miss [*sic*].
How'd you do that?"
the cops said.

574

As she told me about her ruined belongings, she professed annoyance. But her irises rippled green and her mouth lifted up, and when she said "laptop," wrinkles skied from her eyes.

---

38 This happened: https://www.history.com/this-day-in-history/lascaux-cave-paintings-discovered.

39 Then didn't: https://www.nytimes.com/1995/03/31/obituaries/marcel-ravidat-is-dead-at-72-found-lascaux-cave-paintings.html.

40 Yes. Amundsen skied out in front: "'Halt!'" Roland Huntford, *The Last Place on Earth* (New York: Modern Library Paperback Edition, 1999), 468.

77

There's a line in *The Information*.
I know, Martin Amis, but that's where it is. "But animals are what they break their silence for."[41]

Hi, Daddy, Dad says.
Bye, Momma, says Mom.
Puppy, says the baby. Pup. Doggie. Dog.

416

And again, Jack lolled his tongue and trotted happily. When the gate closed behind him, he attacked.

575

When you were little, you once ate a dresser. You took the trouble to tip it over and gnaw from the top.

---

41   I remembered this wrong. It's in *London Fields*.

Martin Amis, *London Fields* (New York: First Vintage International Edition, 1991), 97.

78

When I was eight my childhood dog stole my toothbrush. It was part of a game called Sprint the Yard. Oh, good thief, be as thievish as my dog.

415

Jack had stretched over the fence and closed his mouth on me. I went home to check the wound, then my doorbell sounded. Jack had gotten back out. "Sir [*sic*], can you help again?"

576

It's a couple days since that party now, and it's still the same day — the day you died.

79

Now I'm thinking about my friends in categories. Of my friends, not even the cigarette thieves are dogs.

414

I pushed a cinder block against the gate. Just then my head hurt.

577

The barista — not the birthday one or the Staffordshire one, a science fiction writer — talks to me for twenty minutes about a dog.

The barista (not the birthday one or the Staffordshire one — a science fiction writer) talks to me for twenty minutes about a dog.

(&&&)

80

Except I'm laughing now and thinking of Rosalind.[42] She presents like the stateliest of stately. You think: *She'll be haughty. Have I showered myself?* And then there she is, with her cockney rhyming slang and her cheap wine and her great iambic beating heart. There she pretzels on the floor, reading sonnets upside down. I don't mean she can't freeze out her enemies. She has and will. Like a Shiba. Regal.

413

He went gladly — tail up and trotting. Then I shut the gate, and he whipped around at the sound of the latch.

578

She says that at parties she chooses an animal and follows it wherever it goes. That's the way I want to party. Lots of kitchen lots of sofa lots of rug.

---

42   Not a thief: She leaves often, rarely takes.

81

I forgot for a minute that my dog died. I reach down to scrunch
her neck: empty
hand.

412

"Okay. C'mon, Jack," I said briskly. Jack followed me to the back
of the neighbor's house, into the yard.

579

And there's something about the whole unselfconsciousness
of it all. Consciously following a beast that goes just where it
wants.

82

For a minute I forgot what I was doing, which means I left my lost self open and came to light. I thought:

I am wasting my minute here. Then I thought:

411

Jack was outside snarling, slinking: a wolf again.

580

When I was little, what my childhood dog wanted was to sit in everyone's lap simultaneously. She was too short to reach then too heavy to hold but we bore her so lightly — how heavy's a dog?

83

If I write in this backwards, who will I find?

410

"Ma'am [*sic*]," they said. "Can you help us? Do you have any pull with the neighbor's dog?"

581

We'd shut her up — shut her up — in the bedroom. I wish that we hadn't. Barking. Whine.

84

I think it is time for some funeral research. I mean burial. Can I be buried next to my dog?[43]

409

One day during the summer my doorbell buzzed. Outside on the sidewalk: three cops.

582

Something about that, now, makes me despondent. The dog in the bedroom saying look at me sniff my scent, while down the hall a group of people waved group-of-people smells.

---

43 "In an Israeli burial site [from over 10,000 years ago] the hand of a deceased human was positioned over the body of a puppy..." Miklósi et al., *The Dog: A Natural History*, 26.

85

I don't want to die early or to move her or her ashes. But a head-stone? With a dog hole cut inside?[44]

408

Then he would turn into a monster. All teeth, all id. Hate. To approach was to take enormous risk.

583

One thing I believe — back in the coffee shop — is that public whistling is nearly always a display.

44

86

Shouldn't headstones be tall enough to walk into? Short enough for a human, slightly shorter for a dog?

407

Once I had a mild neighbor who had a wild dog. Jack was gentle until he was behind the fence.

584

Also, dogs should be trained well. It makes them versatile. A well-trained dog can attend any party. A well-trained dog can eat salmon without a plate. A well-trained dog collects occasions to be itself.

87

I thought that my grief was postmodern.

406

But can a dog be a glutton? Eating is part of its job. We don't castigate the garbage disposal for consuming. We hurl out enragements when it stops.

585

Well, last week a person who is dating the person I love began traveling twice a day up and down my street.

88

But really: How postmodern is a dog?

405

When a dog joins the family, it acquires the glutton role. All our greed, all our hunger displaced.

586

They may have always been doing that. But now I see: air displaced air displaced air displaced.

89

Don Quixote is postmodern, despite being premodern. The second part a postmortem of the first.

404

In a family — have you noticed? One person's more hungry. The disposal that removes leftovers, the cookie suck.

587

No one in this story is doing anyone wrong, and I respect this quiet, traveler. Nonetheless.

90

All those bulls of Picasso. They could be dogs.

403

The best kitchens have low counters — good for larceny. Every dog should have the height to be a thief.

588

Nonetheless, when I see their bright hat approach, a growl rolls my throat: This is my street.

91

Now my brain keeps on thinking: *Un Chien Andalou.*[45] Is it many years later? Where's the dog?

402

So we changed love to dogs. Violet's Dog. The Herons' Dogs. You weren't there but we thought of you often — we ate our vegetables in the hammock. Salt and sky.

589

I am tightening [hackles up]

---

45   A film by Luis Buñuel and Salvador Dalí. 21 minutes. 1929.

92

In the bookstore I grew up in there was a postcard about dogs.
Mark Twain[46] was a funny one. HAW!

401

Have I talked yet of the place we vacationed? All the cabins
were named [BlankBlank] Love.

590

my own leash.

---

46   Twain can be funny, but it was Groucho Marx who said:

"Outside of a dog, a book is man's best friend. Inside of a dog, it's too dark
to read."

The February 1954 issue of *Boys' Life* attributes a version of Groucho's
famous quote to "Jim Brewer, Cleveland, O.," but it's generally consid-
ered Groucho's line. Quote Investigator — http://quoteinvestigator.
com/2010/09/08/dog.

93

Can a dog make a pun? There's the backwards word thing.

400

for being gone.

591

My person has left for the season.

94

But no one ever makes a play about Todog.

399

I can't read about you. I've stopped reading. I'm so angry at you —

592

Unreason. To love someone so much and to leave them.

95
My mind is

398
I'm not conscious of any answer to that.

593
This vanished day, longer than life.

96

scattered, like a certain kind of dog.[47] [48]

397

Is she there as an unconscious urge?

594

It's another day — a Wednesday — you died today. This year lasts a week. Where's it gone?

---

47 I am fencing with an octopus,

48 a ghost.

97

Growing up, our yellow Lab had epilepsy. We found out — it was frightening — all at once. She had the frontal lobe kind. Religious ecstasy?

396

When we walk to the park — Grover safe in your mouth, me walking same-paced by your side — is your mother there? Is she memory?

595

There is Tuesday beckoning out from the other side of things like the night that always comes, and disappears.

98

My poor dog.

395

Does a dog have an "other" the way humans do? Was stuffed Grover your other? Was/am I?

596

Have I mentioned this yet? No, I'll spare you the burden.

99
My poor dog.

394
A security blanket is a kind of mother — the kind that leaves you to go spinning in the wash.

597
Have I mentioned this yet? I

100

Have you ever seen a dog eat cotton candy?

393

When a dog has a toy that it takes everywhere — the way you took Grover. What goes on?

598

Oh, never mind.

101

They rip a fluff off, hunker down...

392

fabric, color, texture. Musty scents.

599

Have I mentioned this? I haven't ever had a dog. I did have, I mean have had and then didn't/don't.

102

They look so startled.

Where's my fluff?

They scramble up, rip a fluff off, hunker down...

391

When I think of what I want with the most force, it's usually food, often sleep, sometimes

600

You also had me. If knowing is having. If having is knowing how someone smells.

103

Disaster. The mail came — it wasn't for me. The pet store sent a mailer to my dead dog.

390

I think wanting is the biggest the most.

601

If knowing is paying attention — isn't it? If knowing is having, we had us.

104

Should I be wearing some garment of mourning this morning?
A widow's cap? A widower's veil? A leg-tucked tail?

I pull my ears back. Cover mirrors. Shrink my eyes.

389

A dog is a way to be known.

602

A rejection, today, in an email. The subject line? "Bill and I are thrilled."[49] [50] [51]

---

49 June is over the moon.

50 Hladek's ecstatic.

51 Ike is psyched.

105

Bereavement is bereavement is bereavement. Basket knows.[52]

388

I can't just overwrite you with fresh ink.

603

If a dog had to decode rejection letters, that dog would stop acting doglike.

---

52   Basket died in 1937, which is about when Basket II starts.

Vittoria Traverso, "12 Facts About Gertrude Stein," *Mental Floss*, July 26, 2018. http://www.mentalfloss.com/article/5515291/facts-about-gertrude-stein.

Janet Malcolm, "Someone Says Yes to It," *New Yorker*, June 13 & 20, 2005, 155.

106

I need to learn more about famous dogs.

387

Oh so wrong they were so wrong. It's been hours, my lips thought-shaped. Not years. Not months or days. No, never weeks.

604

Why say biscuit when your pocket is empty?

107

Okay, here's a list of remarkable dogs, or, instead, in their absence, a table:[53]

386

You need a new dog, my friend, an acquaintance told me.

605

---

53   There are too many, and every day more of them. Please see Wikipedia for the dogs:

Wikipedia contributors, "List of individual dogs," *Wikipedia, the Free Encyclopedia*. https://en.wikipedia.org/wiki/List_of_individual_dogs.

108

If I could, I would trade places

385

well.

606

A friend tonight, waiting for the same bus. And another friend with her. We ride home together.

109

with my dead dog. At the seaside: cloudless sky acrid smell sloping waves slippery weeds placid sand. No birds in my sight, but you see one. Whimper, point.

384

But when I play dead it goes —

607

She sends me a text about getting together the next week. Let's meet at 5:44, she writes.

110

It's what I miss most: what I miss.

383

wake up.

608

Okay?

111

I told a friend I couldn't stop writing about you. My friend looked at me strangely: What dog?

382

I can't sleep. I can't —

609

Now I'm thinking about dogs and about timing. The nose pushed in my face, waking me up every morning until the clocks fell back.

112

Who can tell about this idea of aboutness. In the coffee shop, Jimi Hendrix is playing "The Star-Spangled Banner." Feedback: Genius is refusal to not be yourself.

381

Without you, everything has become harder.

610

Then I pushed her away, *Come back in one hour!* But she never came back.

113

The grade school I went to was shaped like a key — the classroom windows jutted out in toothy triangles. It was named for a Key: Francis Scott,

380

You didn't say.

611

Was that learning? Or shame.

114

which means I cut my childhood inside a pun.

379

Did you hate how they smelled?

612

How often those two things are linked!

115

Or in a homonym?

378

All those well-meaning soaps in my kitchen.

613

Did I mention I'm reading all these books about dogs? How the hardest thing is to know what dogs know.

116

Those were the years my Lab wore yogurt cups on her snout.

377

I've heard that dogs hate cypress and lemongrass.

614

Do I know you less, now that you're gone?

117

My dad would tell the dog this thing about bananas.

376

Could you smell their number?
Each one's rising death.

615

All letters written to absence are love letters.

118

I didn't like when he said it. It seemed somehow unkind.

375

From how far away would you hear their echoed buzzing?

616

All letters written to presence are complaints.

119

Oh, Sam, just because your nose looks like a banana, he'd say...

374

Would you smell them? Could you retrace their flight from rose to flower to mud?

617

Who said that? Stop barking. Sitsitstay.

120

(But it didn't look like a banana, which was strange to me. He was usually so tidy with his words.)

373

At the tulip farm once, where I went with a friend, there were beetles trapped in the bell of a narrow flower.

618

Lie. What's true is this is a love letter. You're not absent, though you never are.

121

...doesn't mean you're one of the bunch.

372

Can you smell the changed color in red leaves?

619

And in your presence I also wrote love letters to you. I found one, yesterday. It was a poem.

122

I wanted to yell out, *It's her snout, Dad!*

371

You, muddy-pawed and hurtling raindrops. The full dog-smile: greater-than sign, visible teeth.

620

The poem goes like this: .

123

And it doesn't look like a banana.
It looks like a yogurt cup.

370

You, covered with mud streaks, smelling like mildewed sweater,
sheep. Your nose twitching to pull in the ozone.

621

My dog died today.

124

For half a year, she used to wake me up for school at 6:00.

369

This town's a trickle, but a torrent is brewing.

622

.

125

Thank you, Sam, I would say, and give her a hug.

368

Do not insult me with this pointless charade.

623

126

They say dogs don't like hugs,[54] but she accepted it.

367

I'm here now, I guess he thought, and the treats are always with me. The near side is now far and the far side is near and what's close is the treats in your pocket.

624

54   Patricia B. McConnell, "Dogs and Hugs, Revisited," Trisha's Blog, *The Other End of the Leash* (website), May 2, 2016. https://www.patriciamcconnell.com/theotherendoftheleash/dogs-and-hugs-revisited.

127

I was little and feeble with dawn-sleep. Then the time changed from the fake time (Daylight Savings).

366

My friend tried giving him treats only on the far side of the lake — at the halfway point. He ate them, but wasn't impressed.

625

128

Sam woke me up an hour early. I tried, very gently, to explain.

365

He knew the treats came from a pocket, and a pocket doesn't
have to walk three miles to exist.

626

129

But my communication, clumsy, sleepy, sweetly firm — it failed
to reach her.

364

Did he have an epistemological problem with the nature of
walking in circles? A refusal to walk towards the absence of
the present self?

627

(All the ways we consume our own space.)

130

She never came to wake me up again.

363

Why was that? A scent? Or a trauma? A collusion of water, rock, and grass?

628

If a dog were reincarnated, what would it come back as?

131

It's just a story. Don't imagine I got over it.

362

He walks the neighborhood gladly: He'll jog fifteen blocks to the pet store. He'll climb three kilometers on a hike. But the last time we looped around the lake with him? He lay down in protest every few feet.

629

As itself, of course, silly.

132

Sam had her own entrance and run of the yard. She'd watch from a front window then dash out through the kitchen and throw her paws across the fence to greet her friends.

361

But only when he's on a long circle walk.

630

I can't believe you had to ask.

133

The neighbors down the street had a large family. Three small girls, I think, or four or five maybe. It's been a while now, there could be one more.

360

with the letters missing. My friend has a poodle who lies down on the job.

631

I come home, lock the door, toss my jacket on the chair — I hear your waking-up sigh, your claws click against wood. I look down with sparked eyes and loppy grin.

134

Every day they'd walk by on their way home from school and
call for Sam, who was hurtling outside already.

359

I'm only saying that a curb is a stop sign —

632

No one looks up.

135

"Hi, Sam!" petpetpet "Okay, see you tomorrow!"

358

You are dead is all.

633

I read recently about how dogs are wired to follow people — their backs. How being faced is what halts their forward progress.

136

They'd walk on, but one day they halted. A brief, low confab. Then the littlest one ran back. "Sorry," she said. "Sam, we have tomorrow off. We'll see you on Thursday."

357

For a dog park of no one.

634

The author tells a story of saving stray dogs that way — stopping them from racing across the interstate.[55]

---

55   Patricia B. McConnell, *The Other End of the Leash*. I'm not sure on what page. I love this book so much I loaned it to someone.

137

"Okay?"

356

In my closet is a tube of fresh new tennis balls I'm saving.

635

Like a game of Simon Says mixed with *Frogger*, played by animals of different species who have never met.

138

Good-bye.

355

I mean the scent left all over my home.

636

Do we love dogs so much because of their longing? The stretch of their leashes. They pine for us.

139

The thin strand of children thinly halted.

354

Could you be gone so long your own scent fades and eludes you?

637

And when we return, they don't punish us. You
are here now, and the joy is so real.

140

"Tomorrow comes on Thursday," the sprig said.

353

Every day, you knew exactly what you smelled like. There was no returning, after a trip, after distraction, to yourself and being surprised by the heft of your stink.

638

Yes, of course some of their joy is in groceries. Oh, these humans with their great bags of food.

141

Four pebbles, or five, rolled together down the walk.

352

I've read that dogs never grow inured to a new smell.[56]

639

But they're still glad for the one placing the bag on the counter.
And now you smell like a free sample: orange slice.

---

56   Horowitz, *Inside of a Dog*, 70–71.

142

The fifth pebble knocked a structure: a woven wire that stretched and ran. Behind that structure was a pebble of a different rock.

351

You've been gone long enough I can't smell you. Almost. This collar. It will happen so soon.

640

I'm still thinking about a dog's capacity for noticing.

143

Do dogs think, exactly? I think of my friend's poodle, who knows when he has mere seconds to eat a cheese wheel or bag of trash.

350

I read about dogs who can sniff — on slides — one fingerprint. I've said this already. Not the print but the scent it leaves behind.

641

What the Baskets must have known about Toklas and Stein.

144

I was with this friend once when she dashed into the hall with recycling. The door was still closing when her dog scaled the counter and devoured an entire bag of chips.

349

Would our world be bigger if it became smaller? A simple walk to the coffee shop's treat bowl contains it.

642

Does a dog feel regret? It must, certainly. For a moment, a second, but no — I don't think — third thought.

145

How much thought, exactly, did that theft cost him?

348

Sleeping. Downward. Tired. Days. Friend. We need you to explain ourselves to us.

643

I can see you right now lean out of longing. I want the squirrel I lunge at it I snap it runs I'm sad look at that Barbet[57] across the street.

---

57   French water dog.

146

Was it planned in advance?

- the chips are here
- she'll leave at some point
- with the recycling
- for fifteen seconds
- THEN I'LL EAT

347

Let's smell last morning's scents. Person, person, shampoo, dirt, water that touched crumb, crumb that touched lip, crumb that touched lipstick, crumb that

644

But there's no self-flagellation for not being faster. No "I should have, but I didn't." *Regrette rien.*

147

Or was it spur-of-the-moment? Chips chips chips chips chips chips she's gone! chips chips chips chips chips

346

Let's fill last night's stomach with bowls of food.

645

You lost something once — a squeaky rabbit.

148

Crunch.

345

Let's go to the park while this yesterday lasts. I'll throw the ball as many times as you like.

646

Was it still lost a year later? The scent must have lingered, even as it hovered over being almost gone.

149

Is it a case of varying attention?

$\text{Person}^{\text{chips}}$ $\text{Person}^{\text{chips}}$ $\text{Person}^{\text{chips}}$ $\text{Person}^{\text{chips}}$ $\text{Person}_{\text{chips}}$$\text{Person}_{\text{Chips}}$
$_{\text{Person}}\text{Chips}_{\text{person}}$ CHIPS

344

You'd be trying to get more of the in-the-car feeling by extracting yourself from the car.

647

And you must have felt something, a corner of absence.

150

Or is his person not prevention, but the point?

[person exeunt]
[devastation]
[attempt to transfer longing to the chips]

343

If I lowered the window further, you'd squeeze through it.

648

That explains things, like your nose at my palm.

151

Is it transference that explains why I'm constantly eating? First I was heartsick in the warbly stomach kind of way.

342

Is a car to a dog about motion? About scent? About lightness and darkness? About breath?

649

We never really took that many trips together.

152

But now I've had steak. I've had chocolate fries cheese curds.
I've had grapes I've had almonds. I've had popcorn eggs butter.
I've had pretzels chips toast. I've had yogurt. I've had cupcakes.
I've had soup.

341

And what of this clearing? Could you live here, do you think?
I can live but I miss the rhythm of person's feet.

650

Does a short row qualify as a trip?

153

I can't have you anymore, not the physical you.

340

And what was it like on your sofa? *There was warmth on my body which was side-of-person's-leg. There were layers of cushion and time.*

651

Can you smell the different smells that are in water?

154

So I eat

339

I live by dark trees with sharp smells and by soil of small scent on a soft thing near other soft things near food.

652

Can you smell how long since the Rottweiler ran the beach?

155

and eat.

338

But where do you live? What municipality? What state? *I live by one Pomeranian, two terriers, three doodles — one male — and a small shih tzu with a cone around its neck.*

653

When I open my book it's always waiting. Retaining words it doesn't understand.

156

I have learned how to lose you in all seasons.

337

My owner, you couldn't say — *this person called my owner?* — *smells like denim and essence of linden leaves. When walking, person's shoulders roll right.*

654

Would understanding be different if it were all verbs, all nouns?

157

Near the unofficial dog park on the college campus, a grey poodle strains at a lilac leash.

336

It all had to do with articulation. You could know, but not voice where you'd been.

655

A direct object? It's the thing you catch.

158

Behind him, thumbing a screen, his twiddling owner.

335

Your tags jangled. I removed them, put them back.

656

What's the subject? Me, usually, for you. You, most times, for me. We are the subjects and the objects. We do the verbs.

159

When I throw you the ball you always bring it to my feet. Because I trained you, and because it's what you want.

334

It's not just place where we can't place you — it's era. Without words, only your collar might date you. No '80s acid-wash, no rumpled '90s plaid. No neons, no pastels, no canvas bag.[58]

657

But how do we do them? Adverbs get a bad rap, their -lys chopped away. You diminished, walking slow like an old man.

---

58   "Society, which the more I think of it astonishes me the more, is founded upon Cloth." Thomas Carlyle, *Sartor Resartus* [1836] (Oxford: Oxford University Press, 1987), 48.

160

You knew you were the one who was faster.

333

The bone was a bone then was gone.

658

Still you trot when your mood is trotty. Trottily you move along. Trot to where?

161

If you wanted to rest, panting, during my shuffle, you would leave the ball farther from my feet.

332

The language keeps changing and people train to catch up.

659

You know what where is. It means, "C'mon, let's find the ball!"

162

There's what is human, and there's a faster thing.

331

At this moment everyone's a programmer. SQL, JavaScript, C++, R.

660

Dogs don't recognize themselves in mirrors, or maybe they just don't give a damn. What dogs notice is the reflection of your tromping feet.[59]

---

59   Horowitz, *Inside of a Dog*, 219. Only, she talks of "tiptoeing."

163

I'm in a different place today, and a guy who looks familiar is saying *yes, sure, okay* to his cell phone. His voice is soft, like a snow-dampened moan.

330

You'd come back and nose the Pomeranian. Roll it over. Play-growl. Play-display your teeth. It would stand on its hind legs to catch your scent.

661

What no one knows, really, is if dogs don't recognize themselves, as in the concept, or if their eyes can't see themselves, as in the object, or if they just have other nouns going on.

164

The woman who works here and writes elsewhere pulls a drink for me. She tells me a story about running the stairs.

329

A dog in the water. It looks clumsy. Its widening nostrils. Its up-angled snout.

662

What dogs are fascinated with is their planet.

165

When she runs, thinner people shout, "Good job!" at her.

328

Like the whining was a spiral tied to your hands.

663

Have I ever looked at myself like an object? I don't mean have I belittled, have I checked myself out.

166

She flips both her birds up to display her response: full F-you hands that balance my drink.

327

I think it's the same Pom you played with for hours here one day. You kept bouncing into the lake while the Pom circle-whined.

664

I mean, have I looked at myself like a landscape or an abstract? A still life. You know: *nature morte.*

167

I spill coffee on my table the second she leaves it. The brown could be the color of your coat. Can you hear the reverence in the "good job" I say to you and the bullshit in those runners' condescending tone? I said can you. I mean did you. "Be not unrested!"[60] Dead dog.

326

I walk by a couple towing a Pomeranian. They don't notice me, but the Pom does, and back-tugs his leash.

665

Have I seen that shape, have I thought this one? My dimple and nose conspiring to compose a truth.

---

60   James Joyce, *Finnegans Wake* [1939] (New York: Penguin Books, 1999), 26. I'm not done, but it's more fun than you'd think.

168

I think so I think so. I think you can tell. I didn't raise you to be human.

325

Where shall I go now? My first walk without you. It'll be a lot faster, I guess.

666

What's a chin but a *U*, anyway?

169

When I say that last part, I feel confusion. Did I raise you? I guess so. But I didn't meet you until after the beginning. You had eight weeks to be with your mother. You were so small the whole day I brought you home.

324

Does someguy know where the nearest food truck is? Can someguy tell when that jerkhole who fired him is approaching from around a short block?[61]

667

I'm writing this in a kind of a trance. Two dogs walk in, are clucked at, walk out.

---

61 "Towards the beginning of the third year, which was in August, ninety-nine, my uncle Toby found it necessary to understand a little of projectiles." Sterne, *Tristram Shandy*, 110.

170

Back then, you smelled different — like yourself, but less strong.

323

At the park a beagle searches for a yellow ball in green grass and someguy points and laughs at his beagle's blindness.[62] Someguys have a blindness of their own.

668

My approaches aren't always unlike that. I enter, open-mouthed; people emote.

---

62   See the section called "Eyes of the Ball-Holder" in Horowitz, *Inside of a Dog*, 126–32, for details on the reasons (color perception, area centralis vs. foveae, among others) why a dog might have trouble locating a ball.

Not to mention, the dog might be tracking something else.

171

I wonder if adult-you could recognize your puppy smell. This was my blanket, you'd deduce or recall.

322

How can one human ever understand another? We can't understand our own dogs.

669

I roll my smile out for my friend at the counter. She smiles back. That's good. Okay, yes. Good, she'll say.

172

Remember on the beach? You were so tiny. You ran so far away you were a speck.

321

A dog's diary would be written in eternal present:

- eating food now
- cat smells catlike
- eating food now
- drinking water
- this is me i am that smell
- falling asleep

670

But I have to ask her to know if her girlfriend is still in town. I can't smell her stale absence on my friend's skin.

173

Then I lay down and suddenly speck-you ran in circles. Where is stick-you — I will go find him/her, speck-you thought. I stood up, and soon speck-you came careening straight towards me. A speck, a spot, a blur, a blob, you at my chest.

320

671

I don't know, either, that she has stomach pain this morning, or which prerequisite she has for having it. Gluten? Time.

174

The women playing Go keep clicking out their attacks. Six grave heads gulping water, nibbling rolls.

319

672

I haven't noticed how her jaw is tightened, I don't notice that her gait has changed.

175

The game's pieces are shiny: round and bright.

318

                                 stillness

        space?

                                       and

673

And I've missed all the messages that say: I'm alive, I've had food, it's 6:30 but I smell like I do at 6 o'clock.

176

There is more here to say, but I don't know how to describe shape-sounds. How do we recognize patterns? I just don't know.

317

What would it be like to move through various positions never questioning the correctness of your response? Would there be —

674

I put creamer in my cup and walk out by the bushes. Sixteen layers of your memos growing fainter I still can't smell.

177

The guy I couldn't place, or another guy like him, brushed my table and said, "Hey, partner," to my lowered head. "Same chair as always," he wrongly said.

316

You created around you such an aura of peace. When that peace whined for yogurt or pulled at my cuff — when that peace sleep-whimpered — I still felt it.

675

Yesterday, which is today, the day you vanished, I was walking and noticed a rhododendron bush.

178

"No, you're close," I said and pointed, as if he cared where I had sat, and he gestured and touched the table, then stepped away. How did I know him? How did I know I know?

315

And now you're gone and I'm holding these books.

676

You got stuck inside when you were a puppy.

179

At the moment he touched the table I heard a click.

314

You might ask: Whence comes this newfound rigorous interest? I had you for six years, or maybe thirteen, maybe four, and all that time I never wondered.

677

You got stuck the day I took you home.

180

It wasn't of recognition, it was from the Go pieces.

313

I'm not supposed to just write things.
I'm supposed to be reading.
I've bought several books to teach myself.

678

The next day you paused there and lifted your leg.

181

Now he's back at his table saying *orbit-sander* and *Masonite*.

312

You smell thoughts but I always think vision. I have to strain for what you instantly know.

679

It was just a bush now. You were free.

182

I don't know his province but I like his voice.

311

This town is so small and I only notice what I walk into. You smell days-old scents from a half mile away. Your world has many ages, such people in it.[63]

680

Right now there's a man at the coffee shop in line who's so gorgeous he doesn't seem remotely real.

---

63 "How many goodly creatures are there here! / How beauteous mankind is!" William Shakespeare, *The Tempest* (New York: Washington Square Press, 1961), act 5, scene 1.

183

I rarely write her — write here, but it seems as if I'm always around.

310

We went to a reading: We saw one of the locals. Then we went to the park: another one. The coffee shop: another. Then the grocery: another again.

681

His face is so symmetrical there's no friction in it. Like a Yorkie or a Westminster Best in Show.

184

I'm not. It's 6:20. That means food's approaching. Pull your paws off the couch and come along.

309

I spent the weekend with someone who hasn't lived here very long. There are five or six locals they know by sight.

682

He's so flawless no feature describes him.

185

I wonder about those people who chef for their dogs. Beef stew, chicken cutlets, roasted chops.

308

On the side table by the coffee shop's entrance: A toy turtle exists. It could hold a bulldog's interest but never yours. One table leg, though, smells like a schnauzer. And there's a croissant crumb in the corner by the rubber tree.

683

I try — discreetly, from my table — to sniff him, but his scent is so well balanced it disappears.

186

A dog has 215 million more smell receptors than we do.[64] So that blend of dill and cumin, with a coriander lift — it may not taste the way the chef thinks.

307

whatever happens — even the extraordinary — simply exists.[65]

684

In these dog books I'm reading there's so much about language. (Is it language, my face in my hands?)

---

64   Coren, *How to Speak Dog*, 183 (see footnote to section 508).

Horowitz gives humans ~6 million receptors, sheepdogs: >200 million; beagles: >300 million. *Inside of a Dog*, 71.

65   No. Dogs don't necessarily accept deus (or diabolus) ex machina as routine. In West and Young's experiments on dogs and counting, complete with appearing and disappearing treats, "...when the result was unexpected dogs spent significantly longer looking at the outcome of the calculation."

Rebecca E. West and Robert J. Young, "Do domestic dogs show any evidence of being able to count?" *Animal Cognition* 5, no. 3 (2002): 183–86. https://doi.org/10.1007/s10071-002-0140-0.

187

If I taught you to cook ["thought you," autocorrect said], would you privilege volume or taste?

306

we must have observed the ordinary, many times. But for a dog, I think, and I could be wrong here, perhaps

685

Is it language when I bite your leash?

188

You'd savor one enjoyment, or all of them. If our car ride is switched with a walk, your bark sounds happy. When our walk becomes a car ride, your tail wags.

305

To recognize something extraordinary, something in violation of all normal laws,

686

Is this language? I grasp your toy duck.

189

The long maroon blanket spreads out for you in back, but you're in front with your nose against the glass.

304

Ta-da. Can dogs spot illogic? magic? miracles?

687

My friend has suggested when I write about you I'm not writing about the you that I think.

190

On our drive my job is to keep driving.

303

To answer, I would need to disclose your breed.

688

"This is so vague," she says, "no breed, age, coat-pattern."

191

Every stop at the Quik Mart a desertion.

302

From how far away are you pulled to the smells of the park?

689

Where are the dog dishes and the urn?

192

Each return to the car a parade.

301

Is this how you feel when I pause our walks to greet someone?
I'm jawing while frustration eats your leash.

690

She asks about my fence. There's a gap in it.

193

No, do not discount the exuberance, the everywhereness of a dog whose owner has, after so many long seconds, finally, at last, reappeared. Clamber

300

There's the one I want to talk to, and the one I don't.

691

I can't say.

Childhood neighbors of mine almost lost their dog once. This was years ago, in a different state.

194

up.

299

Now I am bouncing on my toes waiting for two people to finish talking.

692

The dog was leashed in the yard and the yard had a fence. They didn't know their new dog was a jumper.

195

That was yesterday, though. Are you calling?

298

I believe so. Food to you is food to me.[66]

693

They were inside cooking pot roast and heard awful screams, then ran out to find the dog hanging.[67]

---

66   Horowitz, *Inside of a Dog*, 43, in a footnote: "Dogs are omnivores who for millennia have eaten what we eat. With very few exceptions, what is good on my plate is good for my dog's bowl."

Also see: FDA, "Good Dog, Bad Food: Foods for People That Are Bad for Your Dog," July 21, 2016. https://www.fda.gov/consumers/consumer-updates/good-dog-bad-food-foods-people-are-bad-your-dog.

67   This dog will make it, but a dear friend's dog didn't. Check your leash length. Check the height of your fence.

196

I can't tell.

297

Your mouth. Would you risk it for the same offerings?

694

The leash was too long. The dog jumped too high. The leash was too short for the dog to land.

197

296

I eat stew with impatience and burn myself. Food with pain is still food. Food comes first.

695

They got there in time, there in seconds. The dog's face was soaking with tears.[68]

---

68   Dogs can cry tears; at least Coren thinks so. See *How to Speak Dog*, 114.

198

I can't tell.　　　Are you calling?

　　　　　　　　　　　　　These worthless ears.

295

Is it almost today? Are you going? The sounds of the street seem strange and small.

696

But he was okay — everything became fine. They raised the fence and he lived nine happy years.

199

Since I've been here, exactly fourteen squirrels fifty-three birds
seven dogs have run by flown by walked past the grey light of
my screen.

294

697

All this time and I don't know what death is

200

Is that what you'd notice with your dog eyes? So much knowledge to be lost and so much gained.

293

Her dog looks in and never stops looking. Like it's staring at a mirror of itself.[69]

698

for you. So long loved. Shaking haunches. Grey face.

---

69   It's probably not. See Horowitz, *Inside of a Dog*, 218–19.

201

How about other dogs? Would I like them? You liked them, I think, even that Maltese.

292

At the coffee shop a large yellow Lab. His owner — she looks like she plays Ultimate! — positions herself at the window looking out.

699

A last lurch towards the squirrel. A leash-bite.

202

Did your days feel too lonely there at home?

291

A downward dog invites stillness or frustration. A play bow beckons wildly for fun. If a play bow is frisbee, yoga is golf.

700

You weren't raging against brightness, you were pulling it in. Another romp, another scent roll. Another ball.

203

I think sometimes of you growing up with me, all alone, like the queer kids who grow up in straight houses, or the deaf kids who are born to the hearing.

290

My grin was finally play bow again.

701

More. Another. And now the little collie is approaching.

204

Is that what it's like? You were adopted. I forgot.

289

There's the smile that offers play and the smile that prevents it. A shoulder jab versus a gut punch.

702

Your friend.

205

I've passed verse 202. I'd meant to save it for Dad's old school song. *Two-oh-two / the school we love.* I will love it, also, on his account.

288

I'd returned to a quality of dogness. There was a kind of bounding earnestness I had regained.

703

I wish I had filmed you in motion.

206

You'd like my dad. Maybe you did like him. You didn't meet him, whichever you you are.

287

My affect would have been strange and wrong.

704

I'm already forgetting the way you walked.

207

Yesterday, I mean today, was a different coffee shop. I wrote, "You'd like my dad." Except what I wrote was, "You'd like me."

286

Only two days before, she'd have told me to go fuck myself.

705

Every something of you is now something I miss. Aggression is and fear is. Teeth are and tail is. And ear-tip. And commissure. And hip.

208

Was today yesterday? The day my dog —

285

"Drat!" she yelled, grinning and shaking a fist. "I forgot what I was saying! Darn you, Conversation Destroyer!" she said.

706

I drop my book, fumbling it down to the coffee-stained floor. John Berger says, "A voice belongs first to a body, then to a language."[70]

---

70   "I recognize your voice before I know in what language you are speaking." John Berger, *And Our Faces, My Heart, Brief as Photos* (New York: First Vintage International Edition, 1991), 52.

209

The proper response to cherry blossoms on trees is to bark until they're blossoms on the ground.

284

I kept windmilling past, and was about to cross the street when I heard one of the sidewalk-blockers yelling. I turned around.

707

Does the you that is you come before communication?

210

When is ground grass? When is grass ground? When will this dust become earth?

283

"Conversation Destroyer!" I shouted.

708

Your tone is your youness, not your words.

211

I'm not asking about definition, but about selection, what we observe.

282

I swung my arms and walked between them like a windmill.

709

Stanley Coren tells a story about a minister who breeds bluetick hounds.[71] If you were a bluetick, would tone change you?

---

71   Coren, *How to Speak Dog*, 194–97.

212

Why orange?

281

710

Here are some of the sighting-sounds hounds make:[72]

Bear
    Zeke: "sort of a growl-bark but not very loud"
    Becky:"she just stands and growls"

Big Cat
    Zeke: "mostly a high — almost squeaky — bark"
    Becky:"a little tiny turn-up at the end of each bark"

Deer
    Zeke: "[...] the real music [...] like proper hounds"
    Becky:"[...] the real music [...] like proper hounds"

Rabbit
    Zeke: "kind of a *yip-yodel* sound"
    Becky:"yips and yodels like she should"

Raccoon
    Zeke: "mostly *yodel*"
    Becky:"yips and yodels like she should"

Squirrel
    Zeke: "mostly *yip*"
    Becky:"yips and yodels like she should"

---

72 Coren, *How to Speak Dog*, 195. Quotes are Coren quoting Brother John, who sometimes quotes his dogs.

213

Because green has been taken.

280

One day I was walking down Pine Street, almost myself again. Two people were conversing, blocking my path.

711

Please tell me. Is this language? Is it instinct? Is it visceral reaction to different smells?

214

I'm reading John Berger's *And Our Faces, My Heart, Brief as Photos*. He talks about a white kitten in a white room that sleeps against white. "I have always thought that household gods were animals," Berger says.[73]

279

I still remember how it felt when the wall began thinning. Which you are you? I hadn't met you yet.

712

I yell "fuck" when I strike my thumb with a hammer.

---

73 Berger, *And Our Faces, My Heart, Brief as Photos*, 6–7.

215

There is so much beckoning in become.

278

It could have been isinglass,[74] that artifact of Saul and F. Scott.
Whatever it was, it was a thickness.

713

A child yells, "Moon!" when the pale moon, half occluded,
squints out from the not-bedtime sky.

---

74 Saul Bellow mentions isinglass in *Humboldt's Gift*. I could've sworn
it was in *Gatsby*, but it's not.

216

John Berger is another who died the same year you died. He died on January 2, 2017. As if he waited to gain the year, and then waited to see the year, and then waited to brush one toe against a Monday.

277

At the time, depression and introversion made no sense to me. Later, after the loss of an other that was less other than self, I found myself behind a thick Lucite wall.

714

And our scent. It is also communication. The content only partly under our control.

217

"Now you are everywhere," Simon McBurney writes.[75] For you, it was different. Who are you and are you? I hear my friend Laura asking — Where is this dog?

276

a human version must have been too much to endure. Me: "Hey! Hey! How's it going? Lopsided smile!"

Her:

[Grimace]
[Slump]
[*fuck*]
[now we hide]

715

I read about a basenji[76] who would pee upside down, while completing a backflip against a tree trunk.

---

75 Simon McBurney. https://twitter.com/SimonMcBurney. 9:58 a.m., 2 Jan 2017.

76 Coren, *How to Speak Dog*, 187. "...acrobatic somersault with a continuous stream of urine flowing."

218

And yes of course yes just one dog and so many. So many dogs
I have petted, brushed, and run. And yes you are the dog whose
fur obscures patterns on my sweater. And yes of course you
are the dog.

275

While an actual dog might have cheered her saddened self,

716

You were more mild mannered in your habits than that basenji.
A leg lifted,

219

In the coffee shop again/still. Is it a year now?

274

At that time in my life I was doglike myself: giant smiles, vigorous gestures, bounding walk.

717

not overly high.

220

This isn't déjà vu — it's too familiar. I'm remembering something I've never left. *Toujours là.*

273

I learned much later that she'd been depressed for many months. Her dog needed walking, so they walked.

718

And you weren't a big dirt scratcher — no turf parades. No strange divots shaped like a slid paw.

221

I'm thinking again of John Berger and his white kitten camouflaged.

272

She was hiding from me. I am sure of it. But beyond hi we had never conversed.

719

You were content to make your statement and move on.

222

Are you more present in your absence than I was absent in your presence?

271

Once I saw her in the park walking her dog in my direction. She juke-stepped behind a fountain and slipped from sight.

720

At the coffee shop, a Staffordshire bends under a table. It's completely food-focused. Scent and smell.

223

It's a fair question, but really I think not.

270

Many years ago, in a building where I thumbed through my nights, there lived a woman with a punk aesthetic and a gothed-out dog.

721

I once took a ride on a cramped cable car where every rider talked money nonstop.

224

There's the warm fuzz of absentmindedness around you. I am thinking out problems while my hand ruffs your ear. I'm half asleep with my feet beneath your bulk.

269

I don't think we felt that. Not jealous, you and I. Although you clobbered any instinct to be discreet.

722

"That awning is beautiful!"

"$40,000," someone said.

225

Now I'm reading. My hand strokes the couch pillow. Your under-coat still threads into the cloth.

268

The giant dog has been swallowed by an enormous silver truck. Its owner seemed vaguely like he wanted something he never got. That happens to us. We get a giant dog to draw people closer, and then everyone ignores us for our giant dog.

723

"Maybe thirty-seven five. I know a guy."

"Hey! Look at you! Nice glasses. $200?"

226

Always the same question: Which frisbee? Which toy, at the wrecked-grass dog park?

267

Next to the giant, a small child with a furry tail. It's from a fox — *a breed that lives here in the Northwest*, their mother says. *Look how it moves when they spin in circles — like it's real.*

724

Coin focus, food focus.

227

Not the red ball. Against the sad grass it's invisible.[77] Not the brown ball. It blends with the dirt.

266

At the coffee shop a giant dog that can't remind me of you. It's brindled and weighs at least 160 pounds.

725

You weren't like that.

---

77   See Horowitz, *Inside of a Dog*, 128. "Red may be seen by them as a faint green…"

228

Why orange?

I feel drugged today, at the bottom of the lake.

265

A dog is running to jump for a ball in a lake. There's a calculus to that action,[78] Timothy Pennings explains, to how far the dog runs and how far she swims and the angle of her dive into the water. A mathematician can calculate the most efficient trajectory on paper, but a dog calculates, like an outfielder, on the fly.

726

Which isn't to say you didn't know every crumb's location: in my pocket, through the floor cracks, on the Airedoodle's carnassial teeth.

---

78   Timothy J. Pennings, "Do Dogs Know Calculus?" *The College Mathematics Journal* 34, no. 3 (2003): 178–82. https://doi.org/10.2307/3595798. Pennings relied on Elvis, a male Welsh corgi, for his data.

For an argument that a dog's calculations are more fluid, see:

Pierre Perruchet and Jorge Gallego, "Do Dogs Know Related Rates Rather than Optimization?" *The College Mathematics Journal* 37, no. 1 (2006): 16–18. https://doi.org/10.1080/07468342.2006.11922161. This time a female Lab named Salsa was employed.

229

I am waking as fish swim my eyes.

Why orange?

264

Harmonics on the violin left you howling. "Am I hurting you?"
I'd ask, and put down my bow so I could twist the door handle
and let you out. But you'd just sit pretty by the music stand.
"I am singing now. Please continue," I think you said.

727

But it always almost felt like you had other thoughts in mind.
The sofa and how to hide that it had become yours.

230

I can't answer blue knocks.

263

Something here feels important. "False epiphany?" I ask my friend. Write it anyway, she says, just write it. Right.

728

My pants and the people they smelled like.

231

I thought I saw you last night, along the highway. I stopped my car and opened the door. Come in, come on.

262

To my left, one seat over, Hero's owner, holding a brush. She has a dog named Hector, too, and the borrowed cat, Levi. As a cat he lacks narrative weight.

729

The late-night provocations of the neighbor's sounds.

232

I thought I saw you this morning in the alleyway. I crouched low. That brown yellow — was that your tail?

261

730

And the bark and swirl you made when I'd been out and returned. It wasn't food-based. It was

233

In the museum, a sculpture: *Greyhounds Playing*, ca. 1916.[79]
One dog is on the ground, curving upwards. The other on top,
extending legs. Those curving ears ask fluid questions I thought
of you.

260

731

about how we were ours.

---

79   William Hunt Diederich, *Greyhounds Playing*, ca. 1916, bronze sculpture on self-base, 21 x 38¼ x 10⅜ in., Seattle Art Museum, Seattle.

234

It was almost 7:30 and I'd thought of you only twice. Then the sun rose and threw its bones into your corner.

259

Nah.

732

757

And you nearby so still and so moving.

235

258

I'm going to say a thing now that may make me unpopular with the x^{80} US families who own wiener dogs:[81]

733

The coffee shop is playing a Whitney Houston song — the one Gen Xers like to extravagantly hate. I value Dolly's original, but Whitney Houston — her VOICE, asshole. It won't kill you to respect her voice. Your contempt is as dramatic as her melisma. C'mon.

756

And now Maggie, like a tennis ball, gaining speed.

---

80   The AKC lists the dachshund as the twelfth most popular breed of 2018. https://www.akc.org/most-popular-breeds/2018-full-list/.

81   Archie, you are the softest — I know you know.

236

Today I ate a sack of potatoes, a pebble, and three segments of worm. I wanted to understand how it felt.

257

I tell her wolf.

734

And besides, I will. Always. Until I die or lose my mind. You've lost your mind. You died on me.

755

And then I thought of all the dogs that had lived in Maggie's house. There was Jack, the big beast, and a cattle dog, which replaced Jack.

237

I forgot to mention Lassie. That she was a real dog — a real male one.[82] Many male ones, in fact: Pal, and after Pal, Pal's descendants.

256

My friend asks — "Oh, B, just what breed was this dog?" I tell her poodle. I tell her sheepdog.

735

A pause here,[83] to think about life spans among breeds.[84] What I think about is:

754

And I thought about Maggie, this tiny little dog, owned by one of the largest humans I've met.[85]

---

82   "A Dog's Life: The Life and Times of Lassie," *Daily Mail*, January 1, 2011, 61. *Gale In Context: Biography.* https://link-gale-com.ezproxy.spl. org/apps/doc/A245568007/GPS? u=spl_main&sid=GPS&xid=949e1762.

83   While I'm pausing, here's the definition of *melisma*. It's "an expressive vocal phrase or passage consisting of several notes sung to one syllable..." *Collins English Dictionary* (British definition), online.

84   There's a saying: Larger dogs live shorter lives.

85   Not true. For a neighbor, he's normal sized.

238

You don't have descendants. My mistake.

255

I'm still on the ferry but the land has grown close. It rides the railing like the rump on a rooting dog.

736

My friend Laura. She always adopts older dogs. She presents it as being pragmatic.

753

It's okay. "Hey, there, Maggie. Hey, hey, Maggie," I said.

239

Takumi Yamazaki was born in 1964. He voiced Lassie for *Meiken rasshî*, a 1996 TV series.[86]

254

When I pet Hero, I dream I am petting you.

737

Shorter commitments are easier to keep. But common sense cannot cover her kindness. It's a kind act, and a good one. Only thing is, it's devastating.

752

The last dog of the night, this tiny dog bouncing between my knee and ankle. Her owner — my neighbor — felt her leash hop and looked back.

---

86   The Internet Movie Database: IMDb; IMDb's page for Takumi Yamazaki. https://www.imdb.com/name/nm0945726/.

240

The episode list shapes a story:[87]

"Good-Bye Lassie" is episode three.
"Welcome Home, Lassie" is episode twenty-five.

The last episode, "Run Toward the Dream"
— right now that kills me.

253

My friend has two dogs: I pet one, very dear, and the other one
sulks. I pet the other and the first one whines softly.

738

She'd only just saved Elvis from his devour-the-doorjamb fate,
when he started to die. All eighty pounds of him.

751

the way I pet his flank.

---

87 The Internet Movie Database: IMDb; IMDb's page for *Meiken
rasshî*; the page for episodes. https://www.imdb.com/title/tt0168349/
episodes?season=1.

241

In the photo I found of Takumi Yamazaki, he has gold hair and frameless specs.[88]

252

In the book I'm reading, the author talks about *Umwelt*. A dog has a different *Umwelt* than we do. For example, salt heightens sweetness for a dog.[89] What does that change?[90]

739

A dog shouldn't die.

750

I met the curly-haired dog's owner and we talked for a while. She asked if I had kept horses. Something about

---

88 It's the same photo almost everywhere: RangerWiki, Behind the Voice Actors, IMDb.

89 Horowitz, *Inside of a Dog*, the chapter titled "Umwelt: From the Dog's Point of Nose," 13–32. As Horowitz explains, the idea of *Umwelt* originated with Jakob von Uexküll.

90 "Every subject spins out, like the spider's threads, its relations to certain qualities of things and weaves them into a solid web, which carries its existence." Jakob von Uexküll, *A Foray into the Worlds of Animals and Humans* [1934], with *A Theory of Meaning* [1940], trans. Joseph D. O'Neil (Minneapolis: University of Minnesota Press, 2010), 53.

242

I picture him crying as Lassie, or about her — tears spilling behind frameless glass.

251

Your nose pushing into the metal grid.

740

My best friend had a friend, once, who was maybe in — [I won't write this I don't think.]

749

The white, curly-haired dog walking off-leash on campus who ran up to each set of new legs.

243

Once, I decided to spend a day watching the world from your level. I sat in plant beds. I crawled on carpet, kneed the street.

250

If you were here, my clothes would be soaking right now. We'd be out on the bow in the sea spray.

741

The thing that I'm trying to do isn't working.

748

The dog rioting over my friend's couch.

244

It wasn't much different from the world at my level. Grass tips beckoned, and dirt —

249

I'm back on the ferry from Bainbridge now. Rain is draping the seven slanted windows at the front. From my seat the land is obscured by gridded fencing. There is water. There is a rail. There is the sky.

742

This thing that I'm trying

747

The half-interested German shepherd pup.

245

hallowed ground. To accept a thing you first have to choose it.
In the cardboard of a sagging box were three puppies. I could
so easily have chosen someone else.

248

In Russia, a man bred foxes — *Vulpes vulpes* — for domesticity.
In under six decades they were like dogs, household dogs.[91] But
you were no fox. You go back years, in tens of thousands. There
was fire, there were scrap piles — and there you were.

743
This thing that

746

I'd petted five dogs since that morning:

The pit who leaned closer and closer.

---

91   Lee Alan Dugatkin and Lyudmila Trut, *How to Tame a Fox (and Build
a Dog): Visionary Scientists and a Siberian Tale of Jump-Started Evolution*
(Chicago: The University of Chicago Press, 2017).

For another take on domesticity in the fox experiment, please see Ádám
Miklósi, *Dog Behaviour, Evolution, and Cognition* (Oxford: Oxford University
Press, 2015), 359–64.

246

But that's wrong, I couldn't. My hand went straight to you. Three puppies and you were the one.

247

You won't stay.

744

This isn't

745

Yesterday I realized

About the Author

Audio

To download a recording of E. Briskin reading from this book, please visit our website, www.entreriosbooks.com/audio. Select this title and enter the password:

C A N I D A E

E. Briskin recorded at Jack Straw Cultural Center
Seattle, Washington
November 2019